FRED'S STORY 2

RUTH LONG, LPC-S

Copyright © 2017 Manitou Communications, Inc.

1701 Gateway, Suite 349

Richardson, TX 75080

Phone: 1-800-572-9588, FAX: 972-918-9069

rossinst@rossinst.com, www.rossinst.com,

www.manitoucommunications.com

Ruth Long
   Fred's Story 2

ISBN: 978-0-9986601-3-4

1.   Child Abuse   2.Child Neglect 3. Recovery

FOREWORD

Ruth Long understands survivors of childhood trauma very well. She understands the self-blame and self-hatred that come from being treated like you don't count, like an object, like a burden and disappointment, or like you're invisible. These messages are ingrained in the child's head over and over for years, through the speech, actions and attitudes of their caretakers. Fred would understand.

In Fred's Story 2, Ruth captures the conflicts and problems of the abused and neglected child in a vivid yet simple fashion, as she did in the first volume in the series. It is a story for adults, one that can be read by children as well. Setting the story in a circus, then in a zoo, and in the suffering of an elephant, is a wonderful way to draw the reader in, to create empathy, and thereby to teach at both an intellectual and an emotional level.

I feel like Fred is a real elephant and a real person, someone I know, someone whose struggles I have watched and experienced. When you read Fred's Story 2, I think you will feel the same way. It is a story of trauma, suffering, healing, hope and recovery. Fred's story is a moving and subtle dramatization of the conflicts experienced by many abused and neglected children. The workbook that accompanies Fred's Story 2 is a set of exercises that capture much of the work of recovery. I think that survivors will find them useful, and will appreciate knowing that someone else – Fred – has gone through what they have gone through, and come out the other side.

Colin A. Ross, M.D.
Dallas, Texas

CHAPTER ONE

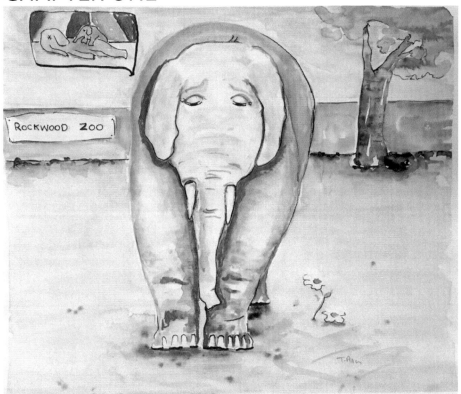

Rockwood Zoo! What a place this turned out to be!

Fred was somehow tolerating his many neighbors. And, the giant monster that sent Fred on his initial frozen adventure was now no more than an oversized bundle of. . . obnoxious. Fred had enjoyed his old solitude back in the cozy circus tent, but this place had its perks too. Others were always there if the boredom began pressing in. However, Fred was careful not to make any consistent interactions. He could have feast or famine, as long as he was calling the shots! He could jump in when he wanted, and then he could jump right back out before he started feeling too trapped. He didn't have to get too close to anybody. . . (And he didn't want anybody to get too close to him either!)

Always cautious, and relentlessly skeptical, Fred wanted to keep abreast of any future changes that could impact him.

The last major change was very shocking. . . and traumatic. And, he had no intention of missing out on any important news that could be overheard from any of the grounds staff. So far, the hottest news discovered was a proposed change in the meal mixture. (Fred had already had his suspicions that somebody was messing with the grub's ingredients.) All Fred could grasp was that this had something to do with a budget cut. Fred wasn't quite sure what that meant, but he had been noticing that the daily portions had tasted a little more drab lately. Dutifully, Fred persisted in developing his detective skills. There was one particular grounds keeper who Fred spent more time around than he had the others. This guy was a talker, was very fond of his cell phone, and was quite oblivious to Fred's strategic presence. Fred was becoming quite proud of his sleuthing abilities. While encircling his prey, Fred's nonchalant poses and facial expressions left his unwitting informant none the wiser of the real mission.

Being in the one-up position was very exhilarating for Fred. He felt in control and at times would revel in his perceived experience of superiority. Everything was going great until, one day, something mysteriously changed on one of his daily excursions. Fred couldn't quite put his finger on it, but all of a sudden he was feeling really uncomfortable! Contrary to all the previous occasions when his camouflaged presence was apparently unnoticed, this time was just the opposite. Fred knew that humans were too stupid to know he could understand their language, but why was this man staring at him??!! Interrupting this perplexing pondering were the strange words being heard from the man. . . let's call him Sam.

"His father died last night?"

Fred stood very still for a moment and then allowed the words to sink in. Saddened by this tragic news, about somebody, Fred thought quite well of himself as he noticed his emerging empathy for the grieving soul left behind.

Suddenly, Fred's stomach began churning as he tried to make sense of Sam's staring at him combined with these solemn words coming out of Sam's mouth. In reflex fashion, Fred tried to dismiss the whole thing. . . until Sam started to slowly walk toward him. Fred felt another freezing episode coming on and was unable to evade Sam's eventual compassionate gesture.

As Sam approached, he stopped for a moment and then gently whispered, "I'm sorry. boy."

Fred remained stuck, dead in his tracks, frozen in time. "My father?" Fred questioned. . . "He's dead?"

Fred sighed in shocked confusion. Fred didn't know how to feel, what to feel, or if he should feel anything at all. The next thing he knew he was swimming in an encircling sea of anger, fear, relief, numbness, confusion and loss. Fred was sure he would not be standing for long.

After a breach of time of unknown duration, Fred managed to get his rotating planet back in alignment. He then managed to move his feet back toward his abode. On the journey home he seemed lost. The next thing Fred knew, he was at his domicile resting on his mat. It was dark again, much like the unwelcomed intrusion of reality. Fred missed his old chain friend tonight, again, more than ever.

CHAPTER TWO

Sleep was hard to find that night. Tossing and turning only reminded Fred of another night's hazardous sleep. His mind was kidnapped by the memory of his final encounter with his father. And this was not a pleasant memory. To the contrary, his father's verbal lashing and physical intrusion were both brutal and abrasive. This was the father that was now... dead.

And, if this wasn't hard enough, Fred again ventured to retrieve his final memory of his mother. He remembered only good sensations from her while they traveled together before his arrival in the world and her leaving it. The closeness he felt with her during that time he had never felt since.

Nothing made sense. For all intents and purposes, Fred had long ago considered himself an orphan. As far as he was concerned he belonged to NO ONE! He was not wanted and he belonged nowhere, so what was so different now?

This man didn't want me anyway, Fred thought. So what difference does it make if he's dead now?

Fred had no answer, only a nauseous sense of finality that could not be swallowed.

"There's no one now," Fred said, trembling.

Before Fred could mutter another thought, one of his least favorite neighbors came bursting through the door.

"Fred, Fred, You just gotta hear this!" Otto exclaimed.

Okie Dokie. . . This ought to be good, Fred mused to himself.

Half expecting the usual edict from the Animal Social Society, Fred braced himself for the newest glorious event announcement. This time, however, Fred was secretly grateful for the interruption and was in desperate need of a little distraction. . . from himself.

A relay race was the next exciting activity planned. Fred attempted to contain his usual cynicism, although he did have some valid objections to the idea. After all, elephants are not known for their flexibility or speed (unless it was a race to the chow line). Fred was sure this handicap had something to do with the SIZE of most elephants. Being extra large did have its drawbacks, but Fred preferred to use the words, "Proportionately Challenged." Needing to get his mind off those pesky voices and feelings inside, Fred signed up!

Something is better than nothing, Fred reasoned.

It wasn't until much later that Fred realized that he had not even asked what he would have to be doing in this relay race. Normally, not knowing what was ahead would have driven Fred to his less than charming demeanor. But this time, he just didn't care.

CHAPTER THREE

Fred had decided to sleep in later than usual the following morning. Of course, he had failed to calculate the odds of this fully coming to fruition. For, in the morning to follow, Fred was startled awake by the sounds of loud noises and frantic neighbors. Each contestant was gleefully on his way to set up for and practice his assigned relay. . . There was no time to lose! (Fred had also forgotten to ask the date of this social event and had assumed that it would not be scheduled any time in the near future.)

The final straw for Fred came when one of his least coordinated peers dropped a heavy clanging object right outside his sleeping chambers. Fred's more common less-than-charming demeanor was now being transformed into an insidious replacement for his calm self. The more pleasant personality had now been banished to the farthest region of the self. And out came the hot-blooded, fit-throwing semblance of a creature much like the Incredible Hulk, on a really bad day.

This was the Fred his neighbors had seen on "special" occasions. They were reportedly in no hurry for another visit, but ready or not, here he comes! In what seemed like the split-second speed of lightning, Fred leaped to his feet and bolted out the door. At first glance, his face appeared to be grossly distorted, tense and fixed. This was not a good sign.

Fred was enraged! He felt entitled to the peace and quiet he wanted, and could not understand why this was happening to him. Was this too much to ask? Fred did not think so. In fact, he felt that this was an unforgiveable personal assault that needed to be answered. . . NOW!. . .

And WHAT are they starring at? Fred questioned.

Curious to Fred, the next thing he noticed was the frozen pose he had remembered feeling himself before. This time, however, everyone around him had assumed the position. Fred was angered at first by the universal response to his presence. But, somehow, this phenomenon was enough to create a pause long enough to break the momentum of escalating emotions. Still angry, Fred methodically turned around and headed for home.

Arriving at home left Fred confused about the flash of time that had now nearly vanished, Fred went back to bed. He still wasn't sure why they would make him get so mad. Simultaneously, gnawing at him in a deeper place, was the quandary of why he had gotten SOOOOO mad. As if another wave of thought had overtaken him, Fred then began to feel a need to sulk. After all, this was not how he wanted his day to start. Fred wondered how people would feel about him now. Would they be talking about him? Did they know the whole story? Did any of that really matter? Fred just wasn't sure anymore.

CHAPTER FOUR

Morning brought a brand new day. The birds were singing. The air was fresh and clean, clean for a zoo that is, and Fred awoke from his blissful rest with grand and routine expectations of a fairly crappy day. He was not terribly comfortable with the idea of relay race practices, but he found a way to talk himself into it. Fred needed to improve his image. You know, he needed to look like a team player.

Fred was also noticing some changes in his body of late, and all the things that came with it. Rumor had it that there were some pretty attractive elephants who would be attending the relay races, and this sparked Fred's interest as well. Fred wondered if his performance in the races just might get one of these ladies to notice him! So off to practice he went, hoping that the ladies would be easier to please than his old circus trainer.

Upon hearing his assignment in the relays, Fred felt a little more assured of his future success. He was grateful for his assignment after comparing the ease of it to the others that had been assigned.

"Piece of cake!" Fred shouted.

"I mean, how hard can it be to knock a ball straight ahead and into the goal net?" Fred retorted.

Sadly, it was not long before Fred learned how hard it really was!

It was that flexibility thing again. Fred knew this might be a problem! But there was an image to mend and girls to impress.

"So let the games begin!" he cheered.

All this enthusiasm was a great start to the practice time, but it didn't last as long as he had hoped. He was getting tired. He was getting tired of tripping. And, most of all, he was getting a really bad panic attack that this just might prove to be his worst day ever!

Never mind about the critical circus trainer or the potential critical ladies in the audience, Fred was becoming his own worst critic! Each time the ball didn't go as fast or as straight as he wanted it to go, he was sure it was his fault. Any time his leg wouldn't bend the way he wanted it to bend, he'd show it who was boss and kick a nearby object, showing it that he would not tolerate any imperfection. The pain would remind him of that!

Fred practiced for hours, not taking breaks, not drinking fluids, and not listening to his own body when it was saying it could do no more. Finally, the coordinator of the event starting closing up the practice area and Fred was forced to stop. Fred's anger, fear and self-disgust were growing without any end in sight. All the way home, limping and breathing heavily, he continued his self-loathing dialogue. Now he was even keenly regretting that he had even entered this stupid event, and now he was trapped! Tomorrow was the big day and Fred felt it would just be easier to die than to have to face it.

CHAPTER FIVE

Ladies and Gents, Welcome to the First Annual Relay Race Competition! It is with great pride that we...

Fred wasn't quite sure how he got to the show tent, but here he was, waiting as instructed for his race to begin. His body was there, but it was no secret that he and his frame were NOT on speaking terms! For with each micro-movement, the pain center in his exhausted brain sprang into throbbing action. And speaking of springing into action, Fred knew too well that his actions needed to be quick and precise. No room for error here!

Distracted by the brightness of the noon sun, Fred turned his gaze to the audience who were enjoying much more of the day's shade than he was. As his eyes scanned the cheering crowd, they fell upon the most stunning of sights, a vision of absolute and pure female elephant beauty.

Who was this angelic creature here to view such physical exploits? Fred wondered.

Fred had never seen this gal before, but he was hooked!

Internally, it felt like Fred was hosting a basketball game, and the ball continued to be dribbled harder and harder until it was masterfully thrown into the net located right in Fred's throat area. . . He couldn't swallow. . . He couldn't move. . . Couldn't Move?. . .

Come on feet, you HAVE to move! Fred demanded.

Despite the many orders, Fred was not able to stop the basketball game on the internal front, nor was he successful in getting his feet to break free from remaining in their hardened place. Fred was beginning to panic.

In an attempt to try and soothe himself, Fred reasoned, Surely there is still some time before our race begins.

Fred had made himself a little more hopeful.

Ding. . . Ding. . . Ding. . . Ladies and Gents, Round 3 will begin in 15 minutes. Grab some peanuts, get some water - it's hot out her - -and don't forget to use the little elephants' room while you can!

Fred breathed a short sigh of relief. He had 15 minutes to pull it together. First, he just had to stop his internal team from going into the second quarter of the game. And, he had to get his outside self and moving toward the starting line.

So. . . How hard can that be? Fred retorted to himself. . . I can do it. . . really. . . I can. . .

Ding. . . Ding. . . Ding. . . Ladies and Gents. . . Round 3 will be starting in 5 minutes. Please begin moving back toward the observer's area. And don't forget. . . the winner of this round will be named the Ultimate Champion!!!

Hmmm, Ultimate Champion, huh?. . . Fred pondered. That sure does have a nice ring to it! I bet that Angel in Disguise wouldn't mind spending some quality time with an

Ultimate Champion!. . . OK, legs - do your thing!

CHAPTER SIX

"Well, look who's here! Hey Freddo. . . you_okay there, superstar?? I mean, like we can still see the stars in your eyes. Just wanted to make sure the spaceship has landed."

Fred was used to similar types of sarcastic greetings. But, he sorta hardly noticed them anymore. Besides, this time he wasn't quite sure his ship had quite landed either.

Overshadowing these quandaries was the booming sound of the referee's last minute instructions to the individual racers. All Fred heard was the penalty for any player who used unnecessary roughness toward fellow players. Each player was then given his own ball and then escorted over to his own running lane. (Fred was happy to see a ball on the external side of things. . .)

Then came the official countdown for the race to begin.

10…..9…..8…..7…..6….. (Hmmm, Fred thought, I used to really love the sound of the countdown. . . especially the returning victory flight!)

5…..4…..3…..2…..1   BANG! And the flag is down!

Out of his assigned starting lane, each energized racer sprung forward, coordinating his speed and direction. Fred's exit from the gate was no less heroic. In fact, he was keeping up with the other players nicely! All of those practice time worries seemed to fade away as Fred continued to keep his "eye (foot) on the ball." Fred looked to his right, then to his left, but always to the goal ahead.

As Fred noted the approaching goal present itself just shortly ahead, and with an explosive maneuver, Fred captures the lead! His victory seemed to be in the bag! Not willing to lose this opportune momentum, Fred continued to push forward giving it everything he had! Fred checked his peripherals. . . still clear, and he was even more assured of his imminent success. Fred took one final glance at the net and the ball in rapid succession and made the final strike. Contact! Good contact with the ball. . . and the ball is. . .

"Where's the ball??!" Fred screamed.

Fred found the ball. It wasn't that hard to find. For in truth, despite the impression of contact, the ball had actually only bounced off Fred's other leg and then. . . stopped just in front of him.

In what seemed like a fraction of a second, Fred heard the cheering crowd. They were on their feet, two of them, giving the winner a standing ovation!. . . But, it was not for him. He was not to be the Ultimate Champion. It all seemed to feel so surreal, sights and sounds became blurred. His ears were ringing. The whole arena was spinning around him.

The real Ultimate Champion took his position up on

the stage, trunk raised to its highest extent proudly waving his beloved trophy back and forth for all to see. All eyes were on the platform... Fred sat bewildered on the field. Somehow he could see his old circus trainer with his typical frown of disgust...

Maybe he was right, Fred thought.

The crowd began to press in around the platform obscuring the center stage. At one point, visibility had improved just enough for Fred to see the figure standing beside the winner, the actual presenter of the trophy... Could it be, there she was, His angel. There she was, and she had chosen someone else! All Fred could see was her proud smile as she faced her conqueror.

Fred just couldn't take any more. All he knew is that he had to be some kind of a master LOSER to blow this chance of a lifetime... with her!... Maybe he should have known.

The walk back home had that familiar aura of failure attached to it. He knew this would happen! Fred was sick of himself... sick of people... and sick of life. His solitary home brought Fred a strange sort of comfort. This was his world, all by himself. It was dark. He could be left alone. He was alone.

CHAPTER SEVEN

Fred slept like a rock. He was just too tired to ruminate any longer on the recent fiasco! Waking up (or should I say getting up) was a different story, however. Fred awoke first to the ray of sunshine creeping through the cracks in the wall. Being not so grateful for the invitation to arise from his comfy position of slumber, Fred declined. Then there were the plethora of subsequent invites from the bustling sounds of humans and elephants outside his sacred walls.

This situation brought Fred a great sense of control over his environment, and he liked that! Fred was just about to fall deliciously back into sweet slumber when an invitation presented that Fred just couldn't pass up. It was an actual visitor, but not of the male persuasion. It was a SHE. Melodious and enchanting could only begin to describe its essence.

Fred's curiosity got the best of him at this juncture, and he was out of that bed in two shakes.

Maybe she wasn't at the relay races yesterday, Fred hoped. After all, who goes after a LOSER anyways??!

At this point, Fred caught himself amidst all his speculations and decided he best answer the door! Fred looked himself over as he edged over toward the entranceway. As soon as he saw his lady caller, he felt his chin drop down as if it had succumbed to the force of gravity. This purely scientific phenomena caused his mouth to be left wide open.

My Angel? Fred stammered to himself. He could barely get the words out.

It was her, and she was here, and he was here and. . . ("Fred! Say something 'ya big lug!" came an inpatient voice inside). . .

And Fred immediately attempted a sheepish smile and a barely audible, "Hello."

His Angel giggled in response and then introduced herself.

"Hi, Fred. My name is Jocelyn Marie. I hope you don't mind, but as I was watching the games yesterday, I saw how well you had done, even if things didn't work out the way you wanted them to, and. . . well. . . I just wanted to say that you did really great!"

Fred was in turmoil again, he could barely believe his ears. He so wanted to just respond to her kindness with some wonderful expression of gracious appreciation, but that's not what came out. Another part of him just couldn't bear the obvious humiliation of someone witnessing that horrible defeat, and then needing to come to his own home and remind him of it!. . .

I wonder if her hero put her up to this?, he calculated. Fred heard these thoughts too quickly turn into words and then spray all over his tender guest.

He was mortified. In a confused disbelief, Fred watched his wounded Angel slowly turn and walk away. He wanted to stop her and say he was sorry for whatever had come over him, for this heartless rebuttal. But he could only observe. . . He had her. She had come for him, and he threw her away. What was the matter with him??!

Fred couldn't make sense of any of this. Part of him reasoned that he just didn't deserve her. Another part cautioned against trusting anyone who wanted to get too close. . . it was just too dangerous! Fred didn't know what to think. All he knew was that he lost her again, and feared he would never get her back.

CHAPTER EIGHT

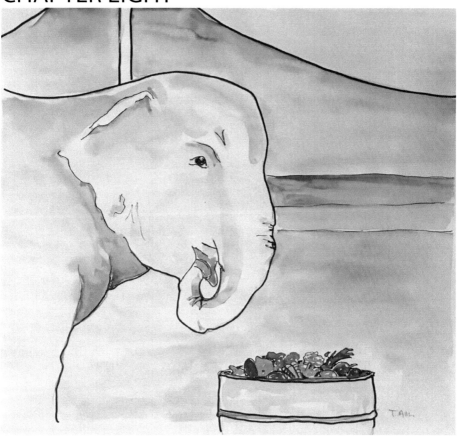

Lunch time! Can't miss that! Fred did have his priorities, and food was one of them. Ah, there was just something endearing about the way it made him feel. If he was sad, he could get really full and think everything would be okay now. If he was worried about something, or even angry about something, the ritual chewing could crunch away any upsetting occurrence. And, if he was lonely (or bored), food was just someone to hang out with and give him something to do.

Fred spent a lot of time alone. He would meander out to the feeding area for fresh supplies. Fred had become quite the skilled concealer, developing a special knack for hiding extra portions on his personage. Once the "crate" had safely arrived at the homestead, Fred would deposit the excess in his storage box, you know, just in case he needed something to tide him over until the next meal.

Avoiding the zoo visitors was a common goal for Fred, but he did make exceptions at times for the little people who seemed a little more tolerable. There were times he would venture out more often - but not so much lately. He missed his Angel, but he just couldn't bear to see her again knowing how much he had hurt her.

Fred didn't like himself much since the loss of Maria. He had lost his mom a long time ago. . . apparently that was his fault too. But. . . he had gotten along this far without a female to love, and there was no real indication to him that this would ever change.

Health-wise, Fred was fading fast. Self-care and appearance were not even a concern. As time went by, he noticed it was getting harder and harder to get around - it just took too much effort. And as far as Fred was concerned, there just wasn't much of anything to get around for! Fred was feeling way too old and tired for his age.

He was alive, but didn't do much living. He was existing. . . just focusing on getting through the day. Once he survived one day, then he would have to figure out some sort of acceptable reason for facing the next one. He wasn't feeling. He had a plan for that. But somehow the discomfort of not feeling was a more cruel taskmaster.

CHAPTER NINE

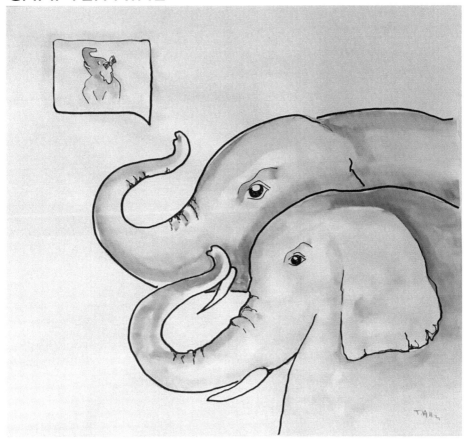

Gossip chains are so predictable, and Fred tried his best to avoid. . . missing out on any of the details. Keeping up with the latest was a lot easier than his old detective gig. Most of the down-low was only somewhat interesting, and there was nothing that related much to him. Something about the shared misery, though, kept Fred hooked on staying in the know.

Fred continued to ruminate over the loss of Maria, and, at last calculations, today would be one month since her "departure."

"Strange what one thinks about on the way to the water cooler," Fred muttered.

He was feeling her loss very keenly that day. . . As Fred

began closing in on the hot spot, he noticed an extra large grouping of participants gathered for the latest newsflash. Fred was intrigued.

Something's up! Fred conjectured.

Moving closer, Fred heard the mumbling. . . and then a name. . . Maria. Fred froze in place and then lunged forward so he could hear better.

"Man, I hope she makes it!" one spectator was heard to say.

"Can you believe the nerve of this guy??!" blurted out another.

Fred couldn't help but cry out, "What happened to Maria??"

"Oh look who wants to know!" sparked an elephant positioned right next to Fred.

"It's your fault, you know! Right after you were such a jerk to her, she started seeing him! She was too broken and just didn't see who he really was. She put up with his angry demeanor until the day he came after her. . . and I heard the doctor say it was touch and go!"

Fred couldn't speak. . . or think. He, like Maria, managed only to turn slowly and walk away. He knew he was not safe there. Each foot of the journey home reminded him that he was not safe from himself either.

"What have I done??!" Fred wailed. "What have I done??!"

CHAPTER TEN

At home Fred paced relentlessly back and forth, back and forth. And the more he paced, the angrier he got. The internal conversation was just brutal. First, it was his father's voice with all of its scathing rhetoric. Right on its heels came the images of the circus trainer's extended hands, always maintaining a cold distance and always replete with looks of dislike, disgust, and disappointment. The worst recall was the final one. . . Maria's face as she turned to leave, shell-shocked, barraged, and unable to make any sense out of what had just happened.

Fred seemed to welcome this experience. Just like the chain of old, Fred found renewed "comfort" in this exercise of memory replay onslaughts. Surely they were justified payment for all he had done. . . and for all he was. . . At least

Fred thought so.

On the physical side of things, all this pacing was giving Fred a whopper of a headache, not to mention the nausea and light-headedness. The next thing Fred knew, he was face down on the ground, but still very confused since the room still refused to stop spinning!. . . Rest is what seemed to follow, but Fred could not trust it, any more than he thought he deserved its embrace.

No one saw Fred at suppertime. Fred not being there was quite unusual. Fred did not miss meals or the opportunity to refill his coffers. Surprisingly, not only did someone notice, but he also came to check on Fred. No, it wasn't any of his own elephant folk. They had neither noticed nor seemed to care. Sam did though. This was the same guy who had showed him kindness once before.

Sam found Fred passed out on the floor with signs of dehydration and heat exhaustion. Sam called quickly for help, and before long, Fred was on his feet again. Fred thought the supply of extra water and snacks was a nice touch, too! Fred flashed back to an earlier time when he was back at the circus, being cared for by the kind doctor.

Fred wasn't quite sure what to make of this second such occasion. He just couldn't understand how ANYONE would even WANT to be nice to him.

Obviously, Fred concluded, the guy must not know that much about me. Because, if he did, he'd hate me too.

Beneath all his anger at himself. . . and the world, there was hurt. Its depth was unfathomable. . . at least it seemed so. There was pain. . . and loss. . . and regret. . . and fear. But these were buried in no shallow crevice. Fred continued to banish them to a very far away place inside to be held and protected by "others." They were just too much for him now.

For the time being, Fred did enjoy Sam's attention. . . and company (and even felt a little sad when he left). He really didn't like it when people left. But this was a secret Fred excelled at, for the most part, keeping even from himself.

As night turned towards its darkest hour, Fred returned again to thoughts of Maria. He hoped. . . and prayed she would be okay.

The medicine he was given was in full effect at this point, and Fred was lulled to near sleep. Whatever was to be would awaken with the dawn. There were grave concerns for Fred, but his eyes could no longer bear the weight of them.

Drifting into quiet trance, Fred heard one final message within him – "Good Night, Fred."

Was it the medicine or the exhaustion talking? Fred wasn't sure who was talking to him, but he didn't want to be rude.

"Uh. . . Good Night. .".

CHAPTER ELEVEN

Rooster crows are quite the wake up call, and for some reason, Fred had his very own rooster well within earshot. It was not a pleasant sound to awaken to, but it was effective. Fred had not actually ever seen the rooster, but the sound effects were undeniable. . . at least to Fred!

Fred felt very grateful for his rooster, a vastly different attitude from other mornings. Somewhere, somehow, in the hours of rest Fred had determined to find Maria. He just wanted to see her and know she was all right

. . . Then like a backhand from an unwelcomed source, Fred realized he had no clue where she was. . . NO!. . . NO! That wasn't going to stop him! It was settled. He would need to return to his old job as Master Detective. Convinced that there must be some blabbermouth ripe for eaves dropping, Fred bounded forward eager to find his love. First stop - the staff mess tent.

Fred had learned from his own species that food and conversation often go hand in hand. Luckily for him, he had arrived at the mess tent just in time. Another good thing for him was that the mess tent was not made of let's say quality craftsmanship. The tent material was also quite thin making snooping a piece of cake. . . (just a little mess tent humor. . .) All Fred had to do was nonchalantly stroll along the sides of the tent and keep his ears peeled!

It seemed as if the stars were all in perfect alignment, since volume was not a problem with this group of workers. However, Fred did have to close his ears for some of their conversation. Humans, Fred knew, could be downright disgusting about their discussions of their various exploits. In fact, Fred had on several occasions felt offended by the term animal being applied only to those walking on all four legs!

"And another thing," Fred began to vent. . .

Fred quickly regrouped himself mentally, reminding all concerned of the mission at hand. He would not fall prey again to any other topical distraction. This was about and for Maria! This was life and death serious! Focus restored, Fred's ears dutifully censored all that he heard, looking only for clues about Maria's whereabouts!

"Oh No! They're getting up to leave!" Fred yelled to himself.

"I need to know where she is!"

Fred's heart was beginning to sink, when at last he heard the thing he most needed to hear. She was in the zoo infirmary at the far end of the compound.

"She's here! Oh Thank God she's here!" Fred exclaimed to himself. Fred was so happy, he could finally get to her. . . and talk to her. . . and then maybe. . .

"...THE FAR END OF THE COMPOUND???" Fred shrieked. "How am I supposed to get way over there? Security was worse than ever and the far end of the compound is a LONG ways away!!!" (Not to mention Fred was REALLY out of shape!)

"NO!. . . NO! There has to be a way, and I'm going to find it," Fred announced to himself.

Fred was pretty shocked with his new Can Do spirit. This part of him was pretty new to him, but he liked it! He was going to devise a plan and leave first thing tomorrow morning!

CHAPTER TWELVE

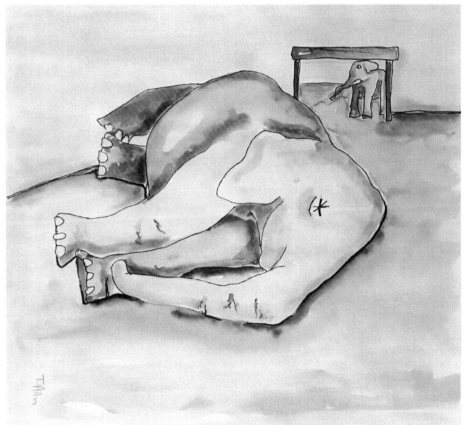

Fred made record time returning home. He was in a hurry. He needed a plan, a good plan, and there was no time to waste! Fred stepped outside for a little more fresh air to ponder the prospects.

"OK, Problem #1, How do I get past security?"

"Problem #2, How do I get way over to the other side of the compound?"

"And, Problem #3, How do I get to see her. . . and get her to look at me when I'm there?"

Problems 1 and 2 just needed a good strategy, a little elbow grease in the logic department. Problem 3, however, felt a lot more complicated to Fred. He wondered if she would even want him to see her. And if she did, would she want to look at him?. . . Fred counseled himself to take one problem at a time. He was content just to find a way to get there and leave the rest for the future to reveal.

There wasn't a cloud in the sky, but Fred was positive that lightning had just struck. For in less than a millisecond, he had an idea! It seemed so simple, Fred hoped. He just had to "borrow" the back of a truck that was traveling in the right direction. . .

"Okie Dokie. . . So much for simple," Fred mused. . ."Wait! That guy in the mess tent, he said he was making a delivery to the infirmary this afternoon!"

"OK, Great!. . . Where is he now?. . . Uh?. . . Oh dear!"

Fred's shoulders were beginning to slump when his ears picked up on a slight rumbling sound - like wheels on gravel. . .

"That's him. . . and there he is!"

Fred ran ferociously toward his prey and noticed there was just enough room in the back of the truck for him. Simultaneously, his internal warning light started blinking as he noted the slight problem of the moving truck. How was he supposed get in there?

Fred's last ride in a truck came with some handy accommodations. There was the wonderful convenience of a RAMP to help make the troublesome ascent. It was also extremely helpful that the truck was in a STATIONARY position! How in the world was he supposed to get in there now??

Fred was closing in on the moving vehicle but was starting to feel pretty winded. It was so close, but HOW. . . Before he could finish the thought, the truck started to slow down.

"Now that's what I'm talking about," Fred cheered.

He was relieved and then ecstatic when he saw the stop sign ahead! And to add a little more gravy to the mashed potatoes (Fred's favorite vegetable), Fred saw the second miracle. There was a huge hole in the path right before the sign. As soon as the back of the truck would descend into the hole, Fred would have his chance to mount the wild bull! And just like clockwork, Fred executed his jump without a hitch (except for the face hitting the bed of the truck part)...

"I made it!... I'm coming for you Maria," Fred chanted.

It was a long ride, but Fred could only think of Maria. She had to be okay. He needed her to be okay!

CHAPTER THIRTEEN

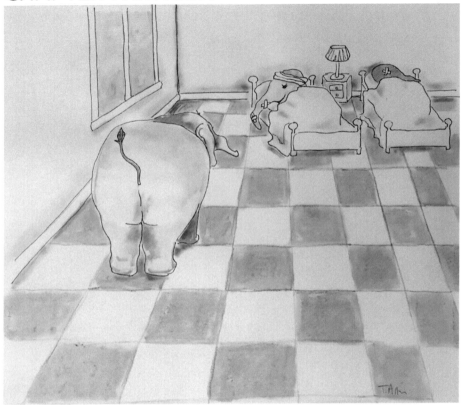

Anticipation had made the long ride seem effortless. For Fred, he just wanted to make things right, and this consumed his anxious mind. This whole experience felt oddly familiar somehow, though - Life and Death in the balance. Would he arrive in time to see his love. . . alive? There was a chill in the air. What if he was too late? What if she did not survive that horrible ordeal??

Fred again felt the urgent pressure within to bury such quandaries. He had to hope. . . he would hope!

As before, the truck slowed down exactly in the right place. Fred could see the infirmary entrance just ahead. It was dark by the time they reached their destination, and Fred was able to exit the truck without detection. He was sore from all the bumps. And, maneuvering off the truck in such a hasty fashion did take its toll. But, the pain from the anguish of not knowing the state of his Angel was all that truly plagued him.

Circling the external perimeter of the facility, Fred searched for some kind of opening, some way to see inside. The darkness was a frustrating obstacle but Fred could not be deterred. Then, when Fred was beginning to wonder if he would be forced to wait till morning in uncharted territories, he saw his chance. There was an opening near the back of the complex that delivery personnel could use to access the supply area. And, the supply area could only be reached by traversing through the main patient ward.

"Perfect! Here we go," he chimed

Despite the large lump in his throat, Fred turned his glance toward the ward floor. All he wanted was a glimpse of her. He had hoped she could see him as well, but first things first. The room was not very occupied, barely any mats on the ground at all. Fred heard strange sounds and saw glaring lights that felt frightening. The urge to run emerged. Part of him began to pull him toward the exit. The struggle was indeed fierce.

Yet, Fred persisted. He wanted to see her. Fred completed his turn toward the mats. There was a larger mat in the back corner that seemed to hold the figure of an elephant. Another urge overtook Fred, and he swept across the room to see. . . His Angel! Her eyes were closed, but she was ALIVE!

As the light shifted to reveal more of her features, Fred could see the damage her attacker had done. He was heartsick! He then intended to quietly turn and walk away before she awoke, but his feet were fixed. And as the light illumined her once slumbering head, he saw her looking back at him.

He had always imagined the first look at him would be one of anger, hurt, and even bitterness, especially now. This was the look he had tried to avoid all this time. Fred did not see bitterness, however. To the contrary, he saw only compassion in her eyes. In an instant his heart melted. He knew he had been forgiven.

By the time the next sequence of lights had cycled, Fred saw those tender and bruised eyes fall back to sleep. Fred did not know why he had been given this second chance with her. But he did know that he would love her to the end of time if she would have him.

The Fred's Story 2 Workbook

By Ruth Long LPC-S, SRT

CHAPTER ONE

Fred enjoyed the perks of relationships on his terms.

What are some perceived benefits of:

1) **Not getting too close to others?**

_____
_____
_____
_____
_____
_____

2) **Not lettings others get too close to you?**

_____
_____
_____
_____
_____

What may be some of the losses in:

1) **Not getting too close to others?**

_____
_____
_____
_____
_____
_____

2) **Not letting others get too close to you?**

_____

_____

_____

_____

_____

_____

- **Being in the "one-up" position sometimes gives the illusion of control and superiority. What are some life events or feelings we may be trying to avoid when we seek a "one-up" or superior position?**

_____

_____

_____

_____

_____

- **Fred was surprised by his reaction to the news of his father's passing. Fred had known only abuse, rejection and neglect from his father, yet the finality of his passing stirred up a huge canister full of emotions. Why do you think this was so?**

_____

_____

_____

_____

_____

- **Describe a similar experience you have had and explore the reasons behind your unexpected reaction:**

_____

_____

_____

_____

_____

_____

CHAPTER TWO

Fred was grieving not only the bad that had happened, but he was also grieving what he had missed (and still continued to miss).

- **What are some of the bad things that had happened to Fred?**

_____

_____

_____

_____

_____

- **What are some of the things you think Fred wished he had now and earlier?**

_____

_____

_____

_____

_____

_____

Fred had the chronic dilemma of trying to distract himself from his own thoughts, feelings, and parts of himself. What are some ways you and others have tried to do this?

_____

_____

_____

_____

_____

CHAPTER THREE

Fred became furious at not being able to sleep in as he had hoped to. His reaction to this disappointment was quite a bit more pronounced than what the situation called for.

How did Fred's thoughts contribute to the "fueling" of this intense reaction?

_____
_____
_____
_____
_____

Sometimes past hurts, that seem to resemble the theme of an old wound, left unresolved can pour into current life events. What "wound themes" in some of Fred's history might have been triggered here, setting up a potential explosion?

_____
_____
_____
_____
_____

What were some of Fred's unhealthy responses to his own outburst once he arrived back home?

_____
_____
_____
_____

Like Fred, sadly, at times when we feel hurt we may lash out at others without being aware or conscious of the effect we are having on them. What are some clues we may be able to identify when our emotions are reaching a critical point?

_____

_____

_____

_____

_____

_____

What are some coping and grounding skills we could use at those times to manage our emotions better and apply better self-care?

_____

_____

_____

_____

_____

_____

CHAPTER FOUR

Pleasing others was a concept that Fred was starting to embrace. On Karpman's Triangle, there are three positions illustrated: the two power positions - the abuser and the rescuer, and the remaining "powerless" position of the victim.

People pleasing to an unhealthy extent can be played in any one of these positions. How might a people pleaser take on each of these roles/positions depending upon the response from the one he/she is attempting to please?

- Abuser: _____
  _____
  _____
  _____

- Rescuer: _____
  _____
  _____
  _____

- Victim: _____
  _____
  _____
  _____

The person Fred found it hardest to please was himself. What are some of the ways Fred expressed this self-critical demeanor?

_____
_____

_____
_____
_____
_____

**People pleasing showed no mercy to Fred. He
literally experienced panic attacks, self-abuse, and
even began to prefer death over the "shame" of not
doing well enough to please his audience.
What have been some of the consequences you
have experienced in your attempts to please others
at any cost?**

_____
_____
_____
_____
_____
_____

CHAPTER FIVE

Fred's body had reacted to both its mistreatment and to the stress it was experiencing. Behaviorally, Fred seemed to be alternating between no action and hyper-action, neither of which was good for his body.

How does your body let you know when it is not in good balance?

_____
_____
_____
_____
_____
_____

Fred also struggled to maintain his internal world so he was able to, in a grounded fashion, meet the responsibilities of the outside world. Both of these worlds needed appropriate attention. Chaos in one often leads to similar chaos in the other.

What are two examples of how Fred's worlds were affecting each other?

_____
_____
_____
_____
_____
_____

When was the last time you struggled to remain grounded and this affected your ability to function?

_____
_____
_____
_____
_____
_____

As your graciously identify this situation, how might you have handled things differently? (This exercise is NOT about being critical of _yourself._ It is about identifying _strategies_ that can lead to an improved quality of life and a better future as you become a more skilled advocate in your own recovery.)

_____
_____
_____
_____
_____
_____

CHAPTER SIX

Fred staked all his self-esteem on his performance.
. . and on one specific performance. This placed
his sense of worth and esteem in a very precarious
position.

How do you relate with Fred on how you
determine your own worth and self-esteem? Do
you base it on your performance, what others do,
or something else?

_____
_____
_____
_____
_____
_____

How does this potential varying sense of worth
affect your emotional states?

_____
_____
_____
_____
_____
_____

Fred also made the assumption that success,
or worth, was only granted to some. . . or one.
He was unaware that these were granted to all.
Fred's unhealthy view lead him to see his peers
as "competition". . . and even sometimes as the
"enemy."

How are you competitive in a healthy way?

How have you been competitive in an unhealthy way?

Fred's past encounters with his father and circus trainer left scars on his heart and filters on his eyes and mind. When it came to the concept of "failure," Fred had some pretty narrow and erroneous beliefs about it.

Can you identify some of these beliefs he had? Feel free to check the box of the ones you share with him, and even add some of your own.

	Beliefs About Failure
	1.)
	2.)
	3.)
	4.)
	5.)

CHAPTER SEVEN

Fred used sleep as a means of feeling in control. What sense of control do you think sleep provided for him?

How have you used sleep as a way to feel more in control?

How had Fred's own perceptions of the previous day's events set the stage for his regretted actions against his female visitor?

Sometimes these misperceptions fuel the enactment of our protector parts inside, leaving us vulnerable to react versus respond.

What are some things you think Fred's protector part was trying to protect him from?

_____

_____

_____

_____

_____

_____

Fred met the perceived "threat" with a counter-attack strategy and ended up deeply wounding someone who was no threat to him at all. Hurt people can hurt people when they have not resolved their own wounds.

Was there a time you pushed someone away or "attacked" them when they were not the enemy?

_____

_____

_____

_____

_____

What insight have you gained since then and/or how did you resolve this?

_____

_____

_____

_____

_____

_____

CHAPTER EIGHT

Fred had learned to use food as a "friend", and sadly, relegated most people to the role of a thing to be used when needed. Emotions were the appointed enemy. Food became the friend that could rid him of any unwanted emotional experience.

In what ways have you used food to medicate or stuff feelings?

_____
_____
_____
_____
_____
_____

What feelings do you try to avoid the most? What do you think would happen if you felt those feelings?

_____
_____
_____
_____
_____
_____

After a while Fred became obsessed with making sure he had enough of his medication and spent a good portion of his day storing it and hiding it from others. The thing he thought he could master, though, was now becoming his master. Isolating was the next response. He was always fearing the judgment of others (and himself).

Share your personal relationship story with food:

_____
_____
_____
_____
_____
_____
_____
_____

Losing someone in the here and now can trigger the pain and confusion of previous losses. Fred had begun to conclude that hoping for change or love was just too painful. False beliefs then came to the rescue "guarding" him from any such hopes.

List some of Fred's false beliefs about his future. Do any of these sound familiar. . . are they beliefs you've adopted yourself?

- _____
  _____

- _____
  _____

- _____
  _____

- _____
  _____

- _____
  _____

CHAPTER NINE

Fred did not feel safe in the presence of his accusers. They believed he was fully to blame for what happened to Maria. In what ways was their assessment inaccurate?

_____

_____

_____

_____

_____

_____

Fred wasn't safe from himself either. He had aligned with his peers' evaluation and became his own judge, jury and executioner. In what ways do you punish yourself for the mistakes you have made or perceive you have made?

_____

_____

_____

_____

_____

_____

How have some of your attempts to punish yourself hurt others as well?

_____

_____

_____

_____

_____

_____

When we do make a mistake, what would a healthy

response to that human reality look like?

_____

_____

_____

_____

_____

_____

CHAPTER TEN

Fred found a new ritual for rubbing his nose in his own self-hatred. These rituals were a strange mixture of "right" or necessary. . . and bad. It felt right to chastise himself for every imperfection and mistake. Yet, the bad side of this self-imposed experience was not pleasant at all. Here again was the baffling attachment to the familiar misery.

If you had just 5 minutes to talk to Fred when you witnessed this behavior, what would you tell him?

_____
_____
_____
_____
_____
_____

Fred had mixed feelings about the care he received from Sam. It kinda felt good, but it seemed so strange. . . and far from easily trusted.

What self-talk do you hear yourself say or think when someone is being kind to you?

_____
_____
_____
_____
_____

Fred had rejected very important parts of himself: the parts that held those deepest hurts and needs.

He was extremely disconnected from himself. What parts of you do you reject, deny, or hide?

_____

_____

_____

_____

_____

_____

What would it take for these parts to be reunited with you again?

_____

_____

_____

_____

_____

_____

CHAPTER ELEVEN

Fred showed great resolve in his desire to find Maria. This was a "newer" (new to him?) part of Fred that he was not as familiar with.

When was the last time you surprised yourself by how well you handled something when the "strong and determined" you was present?

_____
_____
_____
_____
_____
_____

How can you access that part of you more often when the need is great and the "less assertive" part of you could use some help?

_____
_____
_____
_____
_____
_____

Fred, like all of us, can be easily distracted sometimes when the greater need is to remain focused and operating as a unified front with every part of us.

How do you tend to get sidetracked sometimes when there is an important objective to meet?

_____

_____

_____

_____

_____

_____

There is usually a fair amount of ambivalence present whenever there is a difficult task ahead. Some parts of us may have fears or doubts about the intended goal.

How can you negotiate and resolve this ambivalence within yourself so that there is less resistance and internal conflict when moving forward toward that goal?

_____

_____

_____

_____

_____

_____

CHAPTER TWELVE

Fred could have become easily overwhelmed as he began to identify all the issues needing to be addressed and solved. Luckily, he remembered to slow down, prioritize, and take one thing at a time.

Remembering the last time you felt overwhelmed by the many aspects of a problem, what were your strengths and weaknesses as you attempted to resolve these issues?

_____

_____

_____

_____

_____

_____

Fred noticed that, soon after he encouraged and soothed himself in his ordeal, he gained some needed clarity and inspiration.

Describe what happened the last time you received this kind of blessing and reward for remaining grounded?

_____

_____

_____

_____

_____

_____

Fred started to jump from one problem to the next hoping to solve ahead of time all contingencies.

This kind of pursuit or demand for all the answers up front often proves to be more paralyzing than helpful. For Fred, his answer for how he was going to get on the moving truck would not be revealed until a later time when he was already in motion.

What consequences might a tendency toward "analysis paralysis" bring to someone who needs to move forward despite the unknowns?

_____
_____
_____
_____
_____
_____

CHAPTER THIRTEEN

Fred had set out to do the right thing despite the lack of assurance that things would work out as he had hoped they would. It's common for us to judge the correctness of our decisions based on the outcomes of those decisions. Cause and Effect encompasses the belief that if something good happens, we must have done something right. . . and if something bad happens, we must have done something wrong.

When have you doubted yourself or your decision when a negative outcome followed it?

_____
_____
_____
_____
_____

Knowing that the world is not as simple as the childhood developmentally-based cause and effect perspective assumes, how could you re-evaluate the decision you listed above, looking at it from a more abstract adult level of reasoning?

_____
_____
_____
_____
_____
_____

Fred had some urges to run from or avoid facing a potentially difficult encounter that would certainly elicit some strong emotions. He did, however, accept the presence of these fears and also chose to face the situation because the "prize" was worth the struggle.

What "prizes" are you looking forward to as you continue your healing journey, moving forward one day at a time?

_____

_____

_____

_____

_____

_____